EURYTHMY
and the IMPULSE
of DANCE

with sketches for Eurythmy figures
by Rudolf Steiner

Written in collaboration by
Marjorie Raffé
Cecil Harwood
Marguerite Lundgren

RUDOLF STEINER PRESS

The sketches are reproduced by permission of the Rudolf Steiner
Nachlassverwaltung, Dornach, Switzerland.

© 1974 Rudolf Steiner Press,
ISBN 0 85440 278 0

EURYTHMY & THE IMPULSE OF DANCE

I

Eurythmy has been called the apotheosis of the dance, and this indeed it is, but an apotheosis as yet unrecognised by the dance world. Eurythmy is, in fact, that very thing which dancers with a true idealism have been unconsciously seeking since the turn of the century— that inner harmony and balance that was a natural condition of the Greeks, visible in their statues and carved figures, so that, even in a standing pose, movement seems to flow through them. Only out of that inner poise can eurythmists develop and practise their art—an art not copied from vase paintings or reconstructed from ancient records, but created anew by Rudolf Steiner for our time as a system of movement expressing both music and the sounds of speech.

The first public Eurythmy was shown in Munich in 1912 without causing any ripple in the dancing world. But the waters had long been troubled, and new streams had begun to flow when dancers such as Isadora Duncan and Maud Allan (also Margaret Morris, and later Mary Wigman, Madge Atkinson and Ruby Ginner), working separately in their own spheres, tried to bring new life and meaning into the dance. The journey has been a long one and, since the crucial years before the First World War, theatre dance has accompanied more and more the momentum of the times, while Eurythmy has continued quietly to develop its own living art. Meanwhile, the " new dance " or " modern dance " as it is now called, has grown and altered in content—from modest solo performers trying to rediscover the secrets of Nature and of Ancient Greece, to full-size companies with ballets reflecting the chaotic social and artistic conditions which now prevail, the psychologies of Freud and Jung, and also the new impulse towards the spirit which is evident today.

There is Ballet and there is Modern Dance. It has often been said that the former, with its pointes and tendency away from the Earth, has no connection with the moods of our time but rather provides an escape from them. This has never been quite accurate; but now that form of Modern Dance, which has taken root here from America, has brought contemporary themes (whether for better or

3

worse) into the Dance Theatre. While the beauties of traditional Ballet continue to be shown, this other kind of dancing (which needs a different training and technique), comments on the threat of the H Bomb, the pre-occupation of science with technology and its apparent indifference to human suffering; or shows the struggles of bewildered or devastated human beings towards some kind of enlightenment. Instead of trying to get off the earth, to give an impression of weightlessness as in Romantic and Classical Ballet, the Modern dancer is very much concerned both with the physical aspect of the body and with the floor. From flights of lovely dream fantasy the Dance has descended into the cold realms of technical brilliance or the tortuous maze of the sub-conscious and of physical passion. Like many painters and writers, modern choreographers seem often to be presenting the human predicament as they see it, or struggling towards an answer to its problems.

How has the Dance arrived at this stage, widely acclaimed as the expression of this day and age? Why has it descended into this sterile, anarchic state, although for most of the Century (especially the early part) serious artists have been seeking a spiritualizing and renewal of the dance, and in the second decade the new art of movement—Eurythmy—was born? For there is no doubt that in the early years of this Century there was in the air of the world of Dance a feeling for the necessity of renewal; an impulse which had its effect both within the art of Ballet and in the " new art of the Dance " as it appeared in various forms in Europe.

In 1939 the American dancer, Ruth St. Denis, wrote " What are the great spiritual, underlying causes which make the dance bud and blossom at a certain time, what elements in the human economy demand a rebirth?" She was writing about her own experience in Europe in the years 1906-9 when she found such a spirit of renewal, particularly in Germany, where her own dancing was so enthusiastically received that certain people in Weimar were prepared to build a theatre for her, if she would remain there. A few years earlier Isadora Duncan had founded her School in Germany because she, too, found the people of that country the most appreciative of her art. And Maud Allan, the third of these pioneers of " the new dance " had, about the same time, danced her way barefoot across Europe, after a musical training in Germany and a dance debut in Vienna in 1903. In her book *An Unfinished Life* Ruth St. Denis continues " Possibly it (the renewal of the dance) came at this

4

period as a counterbalance to the growing concern with a mechanised world."

No doubt this is true, and much good has come, both artistically and in education, from systems such as those developed by Emil Jaques Dalcroze (rhythm in music and movement), Ruby Ginner (the revived Greek Dance), Madge Atkinson and Margaret Morris (Natural Movement), and later Rudolf Laban (the Central European style of Modern Dance). But, as in so many other spheres where an impulse for renewal was needed, the true counterbalance was given by Rudolf Steiner and came in 1912 with the birth of Eurythmy. But this was not a renewal of the dance as it existed at that time. He viewed the dance as possessing a spiritual origin, and his task was drawing the impulse and creative forces for movement directly and consciously again from that world of their origin. He was not concerned with any kind of synthesis of contemporary trends. That this has not generally been accepted is not surprising since the world has gone in the opposite direction, becoming increasingly technical, material and intellectual. Dance patterns have followed modern trends. But there is in our time a strong impulse towards the spirit—as witness the popularity of Eastern philosophies. There is hope, therefore, that Eurythmy may now begin to take its place in the world not only as an art but as a spiritual experience.

But what, in the early years of the Century, was this feeling of the need for new life in the art of dancing all about? What did these early pioneers try to do? It is almost as though a great preparation was going on in Europe, and particularly in Germany; a preparation whose fulfilment was frustrated by the events which led to the outbreak of war in 1914.

In the last decades of the nineteenth Century ballet dancing had become a matter of technical brilliance and acrobatic fireworks. One reads of enthusiasts sitting in the stalls and counting the number of pirouettes their favourite ballerina was able to perform, or how long she could remain poised on her toes. Ballets were colourful and spectacular, but the music often trivial, while individual dancing had become mechanical and meaningless. A contributor to the Saturday Review in 1892 called ballet dancing a monstrosity and wrote: " The real object has been lost sight of, and mere difficulties made an end in themselves."

It was against this general artificiality of ballet dancing that certain individuals felt called upon to protest. The impulse for renewal flowed from two directions—Russia and America. Within the Ballet itself, in the very stronghold of classical dancing at the Maryinsky Theatre in St. Petersburg, unrest was already active when Isadora Duncan danced in that city in 1905. And it was from there in 1909-10 that European Ballet received a new lease of life with the coming of Diaghilev's " Ballets Russes." The artificial technique remained, but it was imaginatively used as a means of expression blended with " real " music and highly artistic settings and costumes to make an integrated and artistic whole.

But the real impulse to go back to the beginning (which for Duncan and Maud Allan meant Ancient Greece) and to make a new Dance, came from America.

In 1892 Loie Fuller had made her debut in Paris, having arrived from New York a year or so earlier. Her remarkable contribution to theatrical dancing was made in the realm of light and colour and takes a separate, fascinating path. Seven years after Fuller's debut, Isadora Duncan sailed from New York for Europe, and about the same time the Canadian-born Maud Allan left San Francisco for a musical training in Germany. Seven years later again, in 1906, Ruth St. Denis arrived with her oriental/religious dances. The first of these dancers made their reputation and remained in Europe, visiting America only from time to time. Ruth St. Denis stayed three years and then returned to America where her destiny lay. For from the school, Denishawn, which she founded with her husband Ted Shawn, came the founders of Modern Dance in America—Doris Humphrey, Charles Weidman and Martha Graham.

Duncan, Allan and St. Denis all despised Classical Ballet and wished to create an art of dancing based on natural movement and expressing an inner soul impulse. They observed the movements in Nature (Duncan found that all Nature was traversed by a continuous undulating movement) and sought to reproduce them. Duncan and Allan studied the figures on Greek vases and freizes, and tried to discover from ancient records how the dance had been used in Ancient Greece. But their primary inspiration was in music. Maud Allan was a trained musician before she turned to dancing. Some of her dances she created by weaving musical harmonies between the poses which she copied from Greek vases, so as to make a flowing, rhythmical whole. In her efforts to rediscover " the beautiful Mother of the Dance " she even fancied that she had once danced in Sicily, in the groves of Syracuse, before the Christian era, and that the memory of these dances had re-awakened in her a longing to express in movement the emotions aroused by the beauties of art and nature. When she used a particular piece of music she sought first the meaning within the music and then worked out her dance-interpretation of that meaning. But her final inspiration always came from the music itself as she danced, so that no two performances of the same piece were ever exactly alike. Such dancing required very little technique, being a more or less spontaneous response to the moods of the music.

Ruth St. Denis felt herself akin to Nature and waxed lyrical about wind-blown cornfields and the like: she, too, wished to open up new worlds for the dance. But her impulse was strongly religious, even metaphysical, and developed into the exposition of Oriental (later Christian) ideas in strongly evocative stage pictures. What she presented was her idea of the colour and mystery of the East. In contrast to Allan and Duncan in their flimsy Greek tunics, St. Denis wore gorgeous colours and materials, and set her scenes realistically. Her dances bore such exotic titles as White Jade, Black and Gold Sari, Kwannon, Radha, Incense. In spite of a suggestion of superficiality there seems to have been great sincerity and something nun-like about her approach. She dedicated herself and her dancing to becoming " a rhythmic and impersonal instrument of spiritual revelation." Instead of making her devotions within the enclosed convent, she made them, in her own way, in the public theatre, and always she felt that the temple (although it would have been a pseudo-Californian one) rather than the theatre was the right place for her religious dances.

But it was Isadora Duncan who was the most significant of these dancers and who had the greatest influence on Modern Dance. One feels indeed that hers is the key figure in the whole development of Dance in Europe. Many later exponents of Modern Dance look back to her for their beginnings, and already, long before the first appearance of Eurythmy, she had established in Europe her pseudo-Greek style of dancing; it became familiar to audiences as " the new dance " and many were her imitators. It was the dance of the individual personality, as was the early Modern Dance generally. She herself felt that she had a mission to bring about a renaissance of religion in Europe through the Dance, but taking its inspiration from Ancient Greece.

7

In Vienna, Munich and Berlin about 1904 she presented the Choruses of " The Suppliants " of Aeschylus, she herself dancing while a group of specially imported Greek boys intoned. And she retained her dream of having schools here and there which would be islands of the Old Culture. It was her search for a lost perfection and freedom of movement that she believed had once existed, that led her to Ancient Greece, her belief in the truth and beauty of Greek poetry and the movement of Greek dance as she felt it to be.

But this was not the way to renew the Ancient Mysteries for our time: it only served to set up forces of opposition when the real renewal came about. Nevertheless she was a remarkable person and her dancing must have been extraordinary. In her book " My Life and Dancing " she describes how she sought " the natural cadences of human movement . . . . That dance which might be the divine expression of the human spirit through the medium of the body's movement." She discovered within herself a centre of light in the solar plexus, to which the " rays and vibrations " of music streamed and reflected themselves there. From this inner vision she was able to express the music in dance. " Often I thought to my-self," she writes, " what a mistake to call me a dancer—I am the magnetic centre to convey the emotional expression of the Orchestra."

Like St. Denis, Duncan found her spiritual home in Germany, with its serious and thoughtful acceptance of both their arts. And in those early years of the Century, Munich was one of the most active artistic centres.

At about the same time, while Isadora Duncan was seeking to revive the ancient Greek Dance and Mysteries, in the same land and even in the same city Rudolf Steiner was preparing a true renewal of the Mysteries, not by trying to repeat the past, but by spiritualizing the arts anew. For in Munich he and Marie von Sivers were preparing Edouard Schuré's drama *Eleusis*, presented in 1907, to be followed in 1910 in the same city by the first of Rudolf Steiner's own Mystery Plays, *The Portal of Initiation*. Two years later, in 1912, his third Mystery Play contained beings who performed dance-like movements, which were the first Eurythmy to be shown.

It is a strange situation—a city that had enthusiastically received the new dance impulse—and was also the cradle of Eurythmy. One wonders whether any of these sincere seekers after genuinely new forms of movement might, in their travels, have come across there the very first performances of what they really sought; but it

8

seems unlikely. It was not in their destiny to transform their work by the study of Eurythmy.

But that something great, something more than actually happened, had been expected by some dance artists is shown by the remarks in the *Dancing Times* (February 1927) of the Viennese dancer, Else Wiesenthal, who wrote: " When my sisters and I first began to create our dances there were only three great dancers who had broken with the old tradition of ballet. These were Isadora Duncan, Ruth St. Denis and Maud Allan . . . (None of these) had brought the great redemption of which we dreamed to dancing. We looked for . . . movement entirely summed up in, and one with, music."

Nevertheless these were most significant years for the Dance. It is as though, as the time came for the appearance of Eurythmy in 1912, a first stage in the renewal of existing dance forms reached its climax. The impulse flows now from Germany to Switzerland. War clouds gather, and in 1914 Dalcroze (who had taught his Eurythmics in Dresden) returned to Geneva to found a new College there. Laban (the " Father of Modern Dance ") was already established in Switzerland. Eurythmy was rejected in Germany and found its home in Dornach, near Basle, where in 1914 was laid the foundation stone of the Goetheanum, the centre of the General Anthroposophical Society. This centre was originally intended to be in Munich, but the demands of the city authorities made this impossible.

Fuller, Duncan and Allan continued to dance across Europe for many years, but with the coming of the first World War a period ended. A new kind of dance emerged, still concerned with renewing and freeing the dance, and with the outward expression of inner emotion, but more intellectually based and brought down more firmly into the body. Instead of a " token " technique and rather vague ideas about beauty, the tendency was to explore more fully the possibilities of bodily movement and its connection with the ground, and to free the dance from " domination " by music.

Instead of the new impulse, born in the souls of dancers such as Duncan, Allan and St. Denis, being taken up into the spirit by Eurythmy it sank down into the body. At that stage, at that point of time, it *could* have been taken up, if the destiny of its exponents had led them to Eurythmy; what these early dancers did could have been a preparation to be fulfilled and brought to fruition in Eurythmy. But instead the new dance fell earthward, to develop in its own right

9

as an expression of its time, coming further down still after the 1914-18 war with the emergence in Germany of Mary Wigman and in America of Martha Graham.

If Duncan discovered the soul of Modern Dance, Wigman gave it its German and Graham its American body, in that they both developed an astonishing control, balance and manipulation of the physical body as an instrument for the expression of intense inner emotion.

In 1919 Mary Wigman emerged in Germany (after training with Dalcroze and Laban) as a serious, introspective, intellectual dancer concerned with philosophy and psychology, dreams and the sub-conscious—as expounded in the writings of Freud and Jung at that time. Reviews in the 'twenties describe her art as clever, stark, sad, heavy and tragic. But they also refer to the suppleness and grace of her arms and hands, perfect control over all her movements, her deep sense of responsibility and search for ever higher and purer art. The possibility of an art of pure dance movement without any dependence upon music, but sufficient unto itself, was what Mary Wigman believed in and worked towards. Many of her dances were performed without accompaniment, and for others gongs and rattles only marked the beat. Often they were grotesque—she was not interested in dance as beauty only but in every possibility of human physical movement—and reduced to an impersonal abstraction by the wearing of a mask, as in her "Witch Dance." She wore ankle-length, wide-skirted dresses and danced barefoot. One of her specialities seems to have been a hypnotic whirling at varying speeds the skirt swirling round her at different levels, as in her dance "Monotony" given at her first performance in London in 1928. She founded schools in Germany and the U.S.A., where the technical teaching was based on walking, running and jumping; and she was well-known for her choral dances with large numbers of dancers.

So now, after the 1914-18 War, the lyrical dancing of Allan and Duncan, and the Oriental glamour of St. Denis, were replaced by an acrobatic style, a concern with the physical body, and an intense philosophic or psychological content. The dance in Europe had come heavily down on to the Earth. But still the impulse was there to spiritualize the dance. A brochure about her School of the early 30's says " Mary Wigman considers even more vital than the professional training for dancers and teachers the fulfilment of a new vision. Her conception of the dance, as a form of art, is expression

10

in movement of spiritual experience; which is realised by the harmonious union of soul and physical body."

It would take us too far to follow in detail the developments in America, which need a special study to themselves. The memory of Wigman has faded, but her ideas have continued through her pupils. The dance style of Martha Graham (in some ways similar to that of Wigman) has flourished and still flourishes across the Atlantic, and, since the 1950's, in Europe. Ancient Greece was still evident with Graham, but how have the early ideals of Duncan and Allan changed! In Martha Graham was no wish to discover the manner of the antique dance. It was the psychological content of the Greek myths which interested her, interpreted in modern terms. And the attempt by those earlier dancers to reproduce the movements in Nature was reversed in Graham by her remark (in 1936)* " Why should an arm try to be corn? why should a hand try to be rain? Think of what a wonderful thing the hand is, and what vast potentialities of movement it has as a hand and not as a poor imitation of something else. Movement comes from the body itself; not the movement of the body trying to adapt itself to a foreign element."

She has had a very strong influence on the developments in Modern Dance for many years, and from her Company have come some dancers who have gone farther into the world of technology and electronics to produce the abstract or psychological contrivances of Contemporary Dance.

In addition, the infiltration of Eastern philosophies into the West has penetrated the dance world. Ideas from the Chinese Tao Te Ching and Zen Buddhism have produced Dance Groups which seek to eliminate all influence of the personality on their productions and to depend upon chance or spontaneous " happenings." And in Paris in 1967 was produced a ballet called " Mass for the Present Time " in which an attempt was made to mingle classical ballet and Indian dancing. It was described as a Ceremony in Nine Episodes, and included Tibetan chants and bells, allusions to Yoga and to Shiva Nataraja, Lord of the Cosmic Dance. A speaker accompanied the episodes, the last of which was interpreted by one writer as depicting mankind waiting for a divine power which could transcend the chaos of our times and transform the whole world by the transformation of the individual man.

Thus far has the " new dance " come in its search for life and meaning. In the early years the expression of the impulse for renewal was beautiful but vague and rather uncertain. Now, more than fifty years after the end of World War One, the Modern Dance shows within itself two impulses. On the one hand it has become a clever, cold, heartless expression of intellectual ideas and, on the other, a confused, often obscure searching into human relationships and aspirations. Both these impulses contain signs of a struggle towards the spirit, when they are not swamped by mere technique.

And alongside, largely unnoticed, as part of Rudolf Steiner's world teaching for our time known as Anthroposophy, goes Eurythmy—the art of movement which is also an experience of the spirit. Eurythmy must not be thought of as something belonging to the past that started and failed; but as belonging to the future—something held firm in the present for the time when it will truly become the apotheosis of the dance. And in these days, when people in so many ways, consciously or unconsciously, are seeking experience of the spirit, here is an artistic sphere which is open to all who bring to it goodwill and an open mind.

* *Martha Graham.* Ed. Merle Armitage, 1966. p.107.

II

One of the first things that a eurythmist has to acquire is an imaginative grasp of space. But it is a space different from that of Modern Dance. In Laban's system, for instance, the dancer moves within a sphere containing every possibility of movement within his own reach, bounded by the finger-tips in every direction and the ground which supports him. The movements the body can use in space—forward, backward, lateral—may be performed at three levels—deep (on the floor), high (arms raised upward), medium (between deep and high),—with three degrees of energy—strong, weak, normal—and at three speeds in time—slow, medium, quick. Basic to all this three-foldness is the conception of expanding and contracting movement, outward from the centre of the body or inward from the finger tips. Or again, gestures of the arms are described as " scooping " (gathering up to the centre) or " scattering " (pushing outward from the body).

There is much in this threefold attitude to movement, and in the polarity of the centrifugal and centripetal, which may superficially be compared with similar attitudes in Eurythmy. The difference is

12

that, whereas the experience of movement in Modern Dance is confined to the earth, Eurythmy balances earthly with spiritual and cosmic experience. It can do so because, contrary to the modern dualistic view of the human being as a psycho-somatic, if not purely somatic, entity, it follows the main stream of Christian thought in conceiving man as a trinity, consisting of spirit, soul and body. Moreover this fundamental trinity is reflected in each of its members. In the soul it becomes the trinity of thinking, feeling and willing. In the body it becomes a trinity of interpenetrating systems, the head and nerve system (the physical basis of thinking), the rhythmic system (the physical basis for feeling), and the limb system (the physical basis of will). It is with this threefold organization that man stands on the earth—the cosmos of stars reflected in his head—the rhythmical movement of the planets reflected in the rhythms of his pulse and breath—the strength of the earth giving the necessary resistance for his limbs. For man truly experiences the earth forces—gravity, for instance—not when he lies on it in surrender, but when he uses it for his upright position—just as the child wins the earth when he raises himself from crawling to walking. For the Eurythmist, then, there is no limit to space. He shares the experience of the Indian astronomer who said " Sometimes I put out my hand and touch a star "; but equally he feels himself, in his upright position, related to the very centre of the earth.

To experience space in this cosmic way the right centre of movement in the body must be found. In dancing the movement is commonly centred in the hips, from where a certain freedom of bodily movement obviously arises. But for the free experience of total space the centre must be sought elsewhere. It is the arms which essentially lead man into this freedom, and which are also the supreme instruments to reveal the life of the soul. From the horizontal, which they alone can properly express, they can reach upward into the sphere of lightness, and downward into the sphere of weight—levity upward, gravity downward, with the balance in the middle. Thus they relate man to the universe. But also, in expansion and contraction, they express the life of feeling, which goes out in sympathy or draws together in antipathy, reaching both to the outward thrust of will activity, and the inward direction of thinking. And each of these three—thinking, feeling and willing—can be shown in a threefold way—for example the realm of feeling in aggression, submission or agreement.

13

The original inspirer of modern dance—perhaps unknown even to some of the dancers themselves—is the Frenchman, Francois Delsarte (1811-1871) who was not actually concerned with dancing but with dramatic gesture. He may be said to have anticipated Steiner in basing his system of gesture on the threefold nature of man, which, he said, consisted of life, mind and soul, using life in the sense of activity in the physical world, i.e. action or will. The movements associated with these three fundamental qualities he named—

Concentric—the gesture that contracts inward in thought

Normal—the middle balance of feeling

Eccentric—the gesture that expands outward in will.

Because of the inherent nature of a trinity, he held, like Steiner, that each part may unite itself with the other two. Thus he arrived at what he called a " ninefold accord "—and he applied it to the possibility of movement in every part of the body. Delsarte's ideas were widely taken up in America, and were taught in many schools as aesthetic gymnastics or callisthenics. They influenced the young Ruth St. Denis, Maud Allan and Ted Shawn (founder with Ruth St. Denis of the school Denishawn, in which Martha Graham was a pupil.) Delsarte's " ninefold accord " has gradually been forgotten. It had much truth in it, but it lacked the cosmic significance with which Steiner invested his threefold or ninefold man.

It was perhaps typical of Steiner that, when asked about the revival of the dance, he replied that anyone who wanted to acquire a pure conception of the quality of movement should study the sounds of *speech*. For speech is one of the greatest of human mysteries. It is the human microcosm of the macrocosmic Logos or Creative Word —the speaking of the divine powers in the act of creation to which all religions refer. Eurythmy begins, then, with the more difficult task of interpreting speech in movement—and then passes over to the more traditional and accepted task of doing the same with music.

Every sound of speech is actually in itself an invisible gesture. It is a gesture in the air, but still more it is a gesture within the sphere of the forces of life—the etheric sphere, as Steiner often called it—out of which speech is born. The dance is already there in the combination of the sounds. Paraphrase a piece of poetry giving the meaning in other words, it is no longer poetry, the dance of sounds is gone. The primary aim of the Eurythmist is not to accompany poetry with suitable dance movements according to the *meaning* of a given poem, but to express the dance living in the words themselves. These gestures—not arbitrary but given by the poem itself—can then be related to the mood and meaning of the poem through the manner in which they are enacted.

Anyone with a sense for language will instinctively feel the different qualities and mobile shapes of the gestures latent in the sounds of speech. There are of course groups of sounds. The vowels express more the inner feelings—ejaculations, arising from sudden feeling, will often reveal the feeling a vowel expresses. Consonants are more representative of the outer world—it is noteworthy that ancient picture writings confined their picture symbols to consonants. Among the consonants one group is formed of such sounds as L-M-R where the sound (and consequent Eurythmy gesture) is continuous, having no beginning and no end. In another group comprising B, D, P, G, K, the sound is cut short and has definite boundaries. These may be called explosive sounds. Breath sounds such as H and F are outgoing, expanding, boundless, and the Eurythmy gesture must express this weightless experience.

It is impossible to illustrate by photographs the characteristic Eurythmy gestures for individual sounds, for the simple reason that they are *movements*, and a photograph can only show one moment in a flow of movement. In this Eurythmy differs essentially from Ballet, which loves the dramatic pose—and hence loves the camera as well. Even the Eurythmy figures printed at the end of this book, drawn by Steiner himself, barely indicate the actual movement, and are principally concerned with colour relations. To appreciate the movement in the gestures they must be seen performed, or—better still—experienced in the actual doing of them. And anyone who does them rightly will at once feel, not that he is performing the gestures, but that the sounds are drawing the movement out of him. The broad vowel Ah—the sound which also opens the mouth to its widest extent—inevitably produces a movement of the arms which opens them out to the wide spaces. O brings an embracing gesture. Ee intensifies the experience of the unique upright poise of man—balanced between the heavens and the earth—through which he finds his essential humanity, his egohood.

Or, to mention a few of the consonants, F calls for a light darting movement which is almost the polar opposite to the slower, deeper, more meditative movement in which M reveals itself. R demands a continuous rolling gesture while T needs a movement which expresses a certain finality—an event has occurred, as when we say " that's that." L is a life-giving sound: life physical and life spiritual. To perform the sacred word Alleluia in Eurythmy is to experience a renewal of life.

To take the sounds of language in isolation, however, important as it may be at a certain stage, is already something of an abstraction. They need to be experienced in their rich interrelation in actual poems.

Naturally all poems must contain a great variety of sounds, but there are some in which one sound so predominates that they may be said to be written in the key of that sound. The two central contrasting poems in Blake's Songs of Innocence and Songs of Experience, the *Lamb* and the *Tyger*, are in effect meditations on two special sounds. The former is shot through with the lively, life-giving sound of the consonant which is half a vowel, L. And the constantly repeated Ls evoke the lighter breath sounds and especially the calming sound S. The latter poem, The *Tyger*, makes tremendous use of the rolling, tearing sound R. It should really be read with even the unvoiced Rs given their full value, as in the Scottish manner. And in support of the Rs we find the explosive sounds such as D.

> What the anvil? What dread grasp
> Dare its deadly terrors clasp?

Moreover the dominant sound of a poem calls out special tones from the other sounds as well. In the *Tyger's*

> In what distant deeps or skies
> Burnt the fire of thine eyes?

the B and F of the last line have an explosive force not to be found in the muted use of the same consonants in the Lamb.

> Gave thee life and bid thee feed . . .
> Softest clothing, wooly bright.

A poem is often also dominated by a vowel. De la Mare has written one of his most poignant poems so strongly in the key of O —especially the first verse—that the sound sings through the whole poem. It is a poem of the reaching of the present into the ancient past, the past embracing the present and the present the past.

16

> Very old are the woods;
>> And the buds that break
>> Out of the brier's boughs,
>> When March winds wake,
>> So old with their beauty are—
>> Oh, no man knows
>> Through what wild centuries
>> Roves back the rose.

It is not only the quality but the sheer length of the dominant vowel that helps these minute stanzas to bear the immensity of time on their backs. Coleridge has observed that in a true poem the movement of the verse becomes the movement of the meaning. This is surely the case in this small masterpiece.

A change of movement in a poem—almost inevitably, brings with it a change in the sounds. Milton's L'Allegro begins with the dismissal of " loathed melancholy " to the darkness of the underworld.

> There under ebon shades, and low-brow'd rocks,
>> As ragged as thy locks,
> In dark Cimmerian desert ever dwell.

The long vowels of the first line set the slow pace of the whole, while the Ds of the last line effectively bar the light of day and seal the doors of the rocky prison.

But then comes a dramatic change in movement and sound.

> But come, thou goddess fair and free,
> In heaven yclept Euphrosyne . . .

and at once we are in the bright world of mirth and pleasure.

These are fairly obvious examples of the way in which " the movement of the verse becomes the movement of the meaning." On a somewhat more subtle level we may consider the sounds of the opening lines of *Paradise Lost*.

> Of man's first disobedience, and the fruit
> Of that forbidden tree, whose mortal taste
> Brought death into the world, and all our woe . . .

The lines begin slowly with the piling up of consonantal sounds and the heavy D and B in "disobedience." Then we have the light F sounds in " fruit " and " forbidden "—we feel how easily the fruit flies from the tree! But the fruit becomes an inner experience with the M of " mortal ": the two Ts of " taste " announce that a mighty event has taken place: then we are led through the dark sounds of " brought death " to the despairing cry on the long vowels " all our woe."

All this subtle use of sounds of course affects us immediately in reading the poem, and at a far deeper level than intellectual analysis can reach. It is the level at which the eurythmist makes his interpretation, revealing the hidden qualities of the sounds. For many people the discovery of Eurythmy has also been the discovery of sounds.

To interpret the sounds of speech in Eurythmy naturally calls for a speaker who loves the sounds and can bring them to life. Side by side with the art of Eurythmy, Steiner developed an art of Speech Formation, which differs from most other methods of speech training in that it takes its start, not from considerations of the physical speech organs, larynx, palate, tongue, etc., but from the sounds themselves. It must be admitted that for most people today the sounds are experienced by the inner ear alone. Fundamentally the speech of poetry has died on to the printed page. There are interesting attempts today to revive the speaking of poetry, but in most reciting, or speaking of poetry in drama, the speaker uses his voice to express his inner emotions. Steiner on the other hand believed that the mood or feeling should be born out of the sounds themselves objectively. He wanted to recover the magic of speech, not use it for private ends. In a true speech process it is the sounds that form the organs, not the organs that form the sound.

This tremendous variety of gesture, given by the sounds themselves, constitutes the palette with which the eurythmist paints in the air. Ideally he himself should become almost as invisible as the painter of a picture, he should be lost in the movement around him. The veils which eurythmists commonly wear are to help this movement to become visible, one might say also to help the eurythmists to disappear.

Not only does every sound in a poem possess an invisible gesture, the poem as a whole has invisible movement, and the task of Eurythmy is to bring this movement to expression no less than the gestures latent in the sounds. This calls for a choreography based on the inner movement of the poem. The poem may live more in the mood of thought, or feeling or will. Indeed the mood may be so strong that the Eurythmist may prefer to interpret it, or part of it, through one or other of the gestures directly expressing a " soul mood " rather than through the actual sounds of the poem (see the illustrations). If on the other hand, as in the examples given above, a poem is " in the key " of a certain sound, the endeavour will be

18

made to bring all the sounds into the mood of that dominant sound.

Then again a poem may be more suitable for one or for several performers, each representing some particular aspect. A given part may call for backward, or forward, or lateral movement, the experience being completely different both for performer and spectator. It is here that a remarkable feature of Eurythmy often astonishes the new-comer. Broadly speaking, throughout their choreographic movements the Eurythmists remain fronting the audience. This is certainly not so as to display their faces, but in order to evoke an experience of all the directions of space. For if, say, a performer moves in a circle following his nose all the time, he experiences (and the audience with him) only one direction of space—the normal forward movement. But if he moves through the same circle while continuing to front the audience, he (and the audience) experience at one moment a forward, at another a lateral, and at another a backward direction. Moreover, it is a fact which everyone can discover for himself, that the greatest experience of activity—of will—comes through a backward, not a forward movement. Thus if two eurythmists are portraying a struggle—say a duel between two knights—the supreme moment, in which one overcomes the other, is when the victor is moving, not towards, but away from the vanquished. This produces subconsciously such an overwhelming effect of superior power that sometimes spectators have refused to believe they have witnessed a backward movement, because they are so conditioned to believing that the victor *must* move forward. It is an illustration of the great difference between Eurythmy and Mime.

Eurythmy approaches the interpretation of music in the same spirit as it approaches speech. It therefore differs very greatly from the Eurhythmics of Jaques Dalcroze with which it is sometimes confused. Dalcroze was primarily concerned with a new approach to the teaching of music, and especially of rhythm in music. But he also felt that a more intimate and artistic connection could be established between the student and any of the arts (whether music, painting, sculpture or architecture) by his becoming aware of the rhythmic movement within it. It was in 1905, at a Music Festival at Solothurn in Switzerland, that his system of teaching musicians by means of movement first gained public recognition. In Germany one aspect of his method became known as " Rhythmische Gymnastick." But in 1912 this form of movement was shown in England

and it was then that the name Eurhythmics was coined for the principle underlying his whole system. In the same year in Switzerland —at Dornach also in the Canton of Solothurn—Steiner quite independently gave the name Eurythmy* to the form of movement he was inaugurating. Dalcroze went very far in developing great fluency of movement, and something like reflex action, or a reaction of different parts of the body, to complex musical rhythms and counter-rhythms. "The nervous system," he wrote in 1925,† " must be so educated that the rhythms suggestive of the work of art may call forth similar vibrations in the individual, produce a powerful reaction, and become quite naturally transformed into actual rhythms. . . The body must become susceptible of emotion under the influence of artistic rhythms and give effect to them quite naturally."

Interpretation of music in Eurythmy differs widely from this aim. Naturally—like all arts of movement—it is deeply concerned with rhythm, though in a somewhat different way from Dalcroze, but it is equally concerned with such other elements as tone, interval, melody, colour and form. For just as Speech Eurythmy seeks in the first place to express the actual speech, rather than only the subjective reaction to it, so Music Eurythmy—or Tone Eurythmy as it is generally called—seeks to express the music itself. Take, for instance, a simple melody. It will have a basic rhythm but in itself it consists of different intervals, through which it sometimes reaches up to the heights and sometimes plunges downward to the depths. But every interval in the scale has a different quality, and therefore calls for a different gesture. The Second gives a feeling of tentative exploration, the Fourth of an achievement, as of a new position won, in the Seventh we are scattered into far spaces, to return home again at a new level on reaching the Octave.

But music goes deeper even than the sphere of feeling. Steiner always considered it as behind the process of building the harmonious human body. A meditative approach to the scale (for instance) will produce a realisation of the way in which it works in the structure of the arm from collar bone to finger tips. From the experience of the tonic in the collar bone itself—the spring and starting point of all Eurythmy movement—we advance to the first

* The h is omitted because in Greek an aspirated *rho* does not keep the aspirate in compounds.
† In *Eurhythmics, Art and Education*, p.56.

exploration of space in the upper arm. Going further, the two bones of the forearm enable us to experience the difference of *major* and *minor* in the third. The fourth brings us to the wrist, the fifth and sixth to the hands themselves, until at last we reach the seventh in the finger tips through which we scatter the disruptive sound of this interval into space; then, in the gathering together of the whole arm in an inward movement, we reach the tonic again, but the tonic reborn at another level out of the life of the whole scale.

One of the main objects, then, of Eurythmy,—it is one among many—is to bring to visible expression the form and flow of the melody. When you have grown accustomed to seeing eurythmists following the actual tones of an air they are interpreting, so that they seem to be giving life to the sound they are carrying about the stage, and then, perhaps, see a ballet where a given step or movement is repeated again and again, irrespective of what the melody is doing, you have the feeling that in the latter case the dancing is out of tune with the music, it creates a discord.

Where there are several parts to be interpreted, as in a duet, trio or quartet, each part will be sustained by a different eurythmist, so that the interweaving of the parts becomes visible on the stage. Where Eurythmy has reached its fullest development, as on the magnificent stage of the Goetheanum,* a whole symphony will often be performed, in which each instrument is represented by two or three Eurythmists. To witness such a performance is one of the great artistic experiences of the modern age.

Naturally Eurythmy is not confined to the interpretation of melodic line. Major and minor, Apollonian and Dyonisian moods, the difference between the various keys—all these affect the style in which the movements are made and the use of space in the choreography. A Eurythmy training is a complete training in music, indeed one of the best trainings because it uses the whole human being. It should ideally accompany all other specialised musical trainings.

There are, naturally enough, musicians who object that a musical composition is sufficient unto itself and needs no interpretation—though musicians themselves are never backward in setting to music poetry and texts which were never composed with any such end in view. Actually Eurythmy restores to music the movement out of

* The Centre of the Anthroposophical Society in Dornach, Switzerland.

which it is born and develops a more intense appreciation of the music itself. Moreover it is an art in which many arts may be said to flow together, speech, music, sculpture, colour. We have today lost the sense for any real union of the arts. We may decorate a building with a sculpture or a picture, but it remains a decoration, a visitor in an alien environment. We no longer create buildings which demand other arts for their own completion, as did the cathedral and the temple. But when Rudolf Steiner built the first Goetheanum—an immense building, mainly of wood, in which an auditorium and a stage were roofed with two interlocking domes— the whole building might almost have been called a piece of sculpture. The capitals of the interior columns, supporting the domes, were carved with motifs which developed organically from one column to the next: what may be called the apse of the semi-circular stage was formed to receive one of the most remarkable sculptures ever known.* The interior domes were richly painted with forms, which to this day, as seen in reproduction, seem to belong to the future rather than the past: the windows were glazed with huge sheets of thick glass of divers colours, carved in concave relief to form pictures through the varying intensity of the light. The building was space created out of form and colour, and that space was to be the home of the Word. It was the first building of modern times—some would say the only one—to express the essential brotherhood of the arts. It was destroyed by fire on the night of the New Year, 1923.

The new Goetheanum, as original in its way as the old, but built of moulded concrete and therefore of an entirely different design, exemplifies externally no such union of the arts. But it is the home of the Word no less than the old building, and Eurythmy remains within it to express sculpture, speech and music in movement—and to associate them with the life of colour.

For colour is an essential element in stage performances of Eurythmy—coloured dresses, coloured veils, coloured curtains, and the changing colours of stage lighting, constantly transforming all the other colours.

But the aim is not to produce a gorgeous riot of colours, however suitable to the piece performed, as did Loie Fuller with her dancers and their long floating veils, but to reveal an inner relation between

* Not yet in position when the building was burnt down and now preserved in the present Goetheanum.

sound, movement and colour. Many people have instinctively felt an association between a particular piece of music and a colour, and there have been attempts to interpret music with colours thrown on a screen. Sensitive musicians have also felt a relation between the different keys and colours. The change from an adagio to an allegro is often experienced like a change of colour. But to find, or to describe, a deeper basis than instinctive feeling for a relation between sound, movement and colour is far from easy.

Steiner, however, used the experience of colour as a means of conveying quality of movement to the Eurythmist. If you stand upright and spread the arms and hands into the horizontal, you have the human figure in equilibrium with equal access to the arc of gravity or weight downward, and the arc of lightness or levity upward. In stretching the arms into the horizontal you have a movement express-ing the mediating quality of green—the central colour of the spec-trum—between darkness and light. But move the arms in a downward arc in such a way that the hands are rounded inwards, and the movement brings the experience of entering the field of the darker colours, blue and purple. You feel the darkness of these colours as surrounding a central core of light.

If on the other hand you move the arms and hands, with the palms upwards, through the upward arc of levity, letting the whole gesture radiate into a backward and outward stretching of the hands, you have an experience of light and energy, which reaches, in terms of colour, through yellow and orange to red, with its active character of radiating from its own centre to the periphery. Such an experi-ence of movement in relation to colour—which everyone may dis-cover for himself—can lead to an understanding of the Eurythmy figures printed at the end of the book.

Some ten years after he began his work in developing Eurythmy, Steiner made black and white sketches—with hatchings representing different colours—indicating the association of colour with speech sounds, naturally the sounds of his native German language. His friend and collaborator, Edith Maryon, who worked with him on the great sculpture referred to above, then elaborated them with the colours indicated, and they were made into small wooden figures in the workshops of the Goetheanum. Unfortunately only the black and white sketches can here be reproduced, not the coloured figures themselves. In these Eurythmy figures Steiner used form and colour to convey the essential quality of the gesture of each sound.

In the outline of the form may be seen the crucial moment which can lead to a creation of the whole flow of movement in the gesture for each sound. The way in which this movement can be experienced—and even discovered—is indicated through the three colours given for each sound.

We have first what Steiner calls specifically the *movement* (Bewegung) of the sound. The colour for this, to be felt as a flow of movement throughout the body from head to foot, suggests the way in which it can lead us into the gesture of the sound. It determines the colour of the dress worn by the eurythmist in actual performance, though it is the experience of the colour which is the important thing.

Secondly, Steiner indicates a surrounding veiling of colour and form which he describes as the *feeling* (Gefühl) of the sound, the nuances of which can be suggested by the colour. It represents a quality in the gesture which can perhaps be likened to the aroma of a flower. This feeling is represented by the veil, which through its colour and movement enables the audience to *see* what the Eurythmist *feels*.

Thirdly Steiner speaks of the *character* (Charakter) of the sound. In this he directs our attention to the way we experience the gesture right down into our muscles, indicating the greater or lesser tension required, the brightness or darkness, the quality of warmth or cold in initiating the gesture, and, in particular, in which parts of the body these intensifications should be felt. These points of the body are indicated in the drawings, and the colour for the experience is given. The colour, however, is not, and cannot be, given expression in the dress worn by the Eurythmist.

Thus in the case of the consonant B, a force sound, we have a gesture which tells of what we experience when we have an imaginative picture of protection, shelter, habitation. The *movement* is yellow. The whole body must express radiance, strength, uprightness. The *feeling* is blue. One must convey the inward-longing of the surrounding distances. The *character* is red. One must show the inner strength within the whole contour of the gesture. So for this clearly defined gesture we have the strong primary colours, yellow, blue, red.

As a contrast to this, in the case of the consonant L, a labial, we are helped into an experience of the gesture through mixed colours, grey, lilac, orange. In grey we have the constant interplay between

24

light and darkness, a fluctuation from above to below and from below to above. In lilac we have the polarity of blue with its inwardness and red with its outward-streaming energy, made transparent by the delicacy of the colour. In orange we have the mobility engendered by the out-streaming qualities of both red and yellow. Steiner describes L as the sound which can evoke an imaginative picture of change, development, metamorphosis.

For this sound, then, the *movement* is silver-grey. The whole body must reveal an upward and downward flow. The *feeling* is lilac, and has a symmetrical, wing-like form. The gesture must pulsate between inwardness and outwardness, between gravity, descending to the earth, and lightness or levity which we experience in the periphery. The *character* is orange. It is to be felt in symmetrically disposed lines of force in legs and feet, chest and arms, and also in the head. The muscular control of the gesture must be energetic and mobile.

These two examples may perhaps show one of the ways in which the eurythmist may approach the figures and learn to deepen his experience of the gesture of each sound.

Naturally in the interpretation of a poem there cannot be a change of dress and veil for every fresh sound. The point is that the experience of movement and colour for each sound shall have become alive in the eurythmist and imbue every gesture. But, as has been said above, a poem is often in the key of a certain sound, which will therefore determine the choice of colour for dress and veil.

In addition to the figures for the sounds of speech Steiner also made further ones representing what he called " soul gestures," expressing such moods as grief, despair, inwardness, merriment, reverence, tenderness. These are also to be found reproduced, but do not call for special explanation. As already observed, a eurythmist may feel these moods so important in the case of a particular poem that he will rest his interpretation on them rather than on the sound gestures.

This short essay has concerned itself with Eurythmy as an art—even specifically as a stage art. But art today is increasingly recognised as a means of education and of healing. To both these spheres, through its very basis, Eurythmy is deeply related, and in both it has developed a fruitful and extensive practise.

The small child instinctively feels the connection of speech with gesture—an association which leads him naturally into eurythmic

25

movement. But throughout his school life Eurythmy accompanies the curriculum of a Steiner School as a reinforcement and enhancement not only of musical and language experience but of many other subjects as well. It educates a fine perception for speech sounds and musical tones. It brings speech rhythms and musical rhythms into the experience of the whole body. It creates a new awareness of forms in literature and music. It develops concentration. It has many exercises for promoting skill in limbs, hands and fingers. It is a social educator, in which children have to learn to be aware of each other in moving first simple, and then complicated, forms in groups. It is the handmaid of geometry, the place where children experience geometrical forms in movement before they become mere ideas. It is the supreme example of a principle in all Steiner education, that *movement comes first*. For it is the activity of the limbs which wakes up and vitalises the experience of the head.

But the way from the limbs to the head is only to be found through the rhythmic system, the seat of feeling, and feeling demands art if it is to be true. A teacher of Eurythmy must therefore begin with a training in Eurythmy as an art. The eurythmic movements must be strong, harmonious and beautiful, if they are to be effective.*

In the sphere of healing Curative Eurythmy works in the first place as the great harmoniser, bringing the powers of the soul, thinking, feeling and willing, into their proper relationship with the three systems of the body on which they are based, the head, rhythmic and limb systems, and strengthening that balance between earthly and cosmic forces through which man realises his true egohood. But it has also many very particular applications. For Steiner regarded the human body as the creation of the cosmic Word. Man is a microcosm spoken from the macrocosm. And because human speech is a reflection, however pale, of the creative Word, speech sounds as well as music (their origin is the same) are in a formative relationship to the structure and organs of the physical body. In cases of specific illnesses, therefore, the organ affected can be reached by the reiterated practise of specific speech sounds and rhythms. But such exercises, like medicines, should be first prescribed by a physician before they are carried out by a curative eurythmist. And the curative eurythmist, like the teacher of Eurythmy, should first be trained in Eurythmy as an art.

Curative Eurythmy also works on every kind of psychological disturbance. It plays an important part in the treatment of children in the numerous Steiner homes and schools for backward and maladjusted children.

The task, and the effectiveness, of Eurythmy in the spheres of education and healing springs from the fact that it is an art drawing its inspiration and its force from a modern knowledge of the spiritual world. Consciously or unconsciously all true art has done this. But in its origins the arts were religious and their impulse and direction sprang from the great Mystery Centres where a conscious relation with the Spiritual world and its divine powers was cultivated. In the process of becoming a free individual, man necessarily lost this connection with the Divine—he had to escape from the pressure of the divine presence in order to become free. Now his urgent need is to recover in freedom, and in full clarity of consciousness, the heritage he had necessarily to abandon. Materialism will only be overcome by a knowledge of the spiritual world as wide, as detailed and as effective as our present knowledge of the material world.

The art of Eurythmy is one of the channels through which the spirit is again revealing itself to human consciousness. It is a path through which man may again find a way to that self-knowledge which is also a knowledge of the universe.

* For a fuller description of Eurythmy in Education see the chapter on this subject in *The Recovery of Man in Childhood* by A. C. Harwood, (Hodder and Stoughton).

Further related works by Rudolf Steiner:—

A Lecture on Eurythmy
Eurythmy as Visible Speech
Eurythmy as Visible Music
Art in the Light of Mystery Wisdom
Speech and Drama

Edited by E. Pouderoyen:—

Eurythmy—articles with illustrations

In the Plates *Movement* refers to the *Dress, Feeling* to the *Veil* which naturally overlaps the Dress, *Character* to the places where *Muscular Tension* is felt. The hatching indicating the colours (not the same in all Plates) are given, where applicable, on the Plate itself in this order from above to below.

1   Ah (as in ' father ')
Movement (dress)   reddish-lilac
Feeling (veil)   greenish-blueish
Character (muscular tension)   red

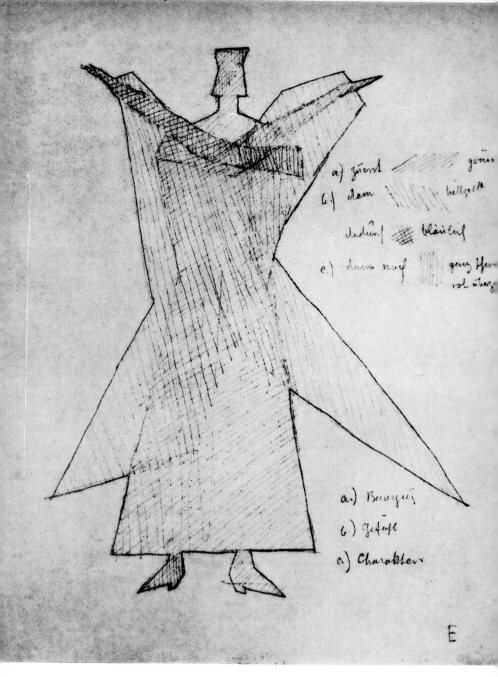

2   E (as in vein)
Movement
Feeling
Character

green
light yellow
pale-reddish

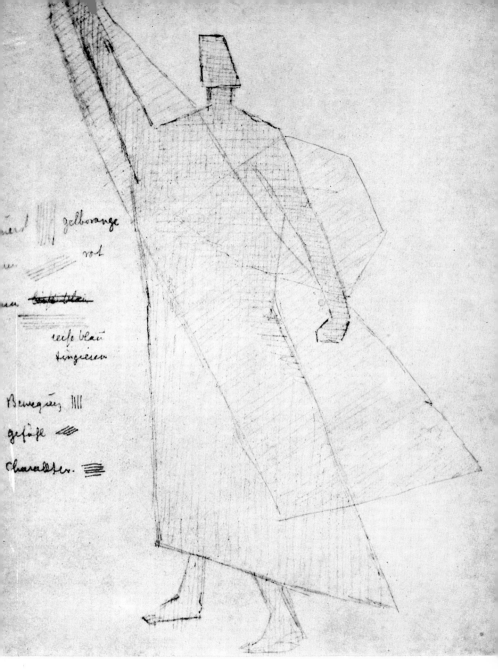

3   *Ee* (as in me)
Movement   yellow-orange
Feeling   red
Character   blue

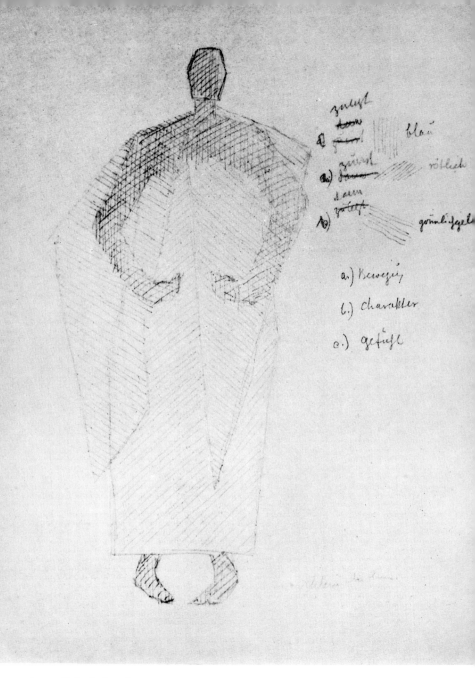

4   O (as in hope)
Movement   reddish
Feeling   greenish-yellow
Character   blue

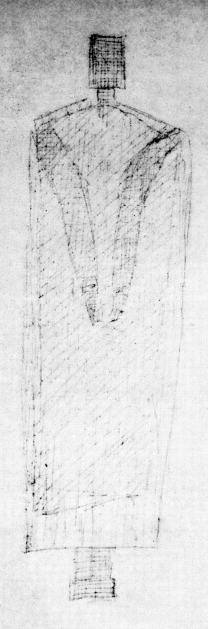

a) zürst ||||| blau

b) dann ///// gelb

c) dann läuft bürgern ≡≡≡≡
                          lila

a.) Bewegung

b.) Gefühl

c.) Charakter.

U

5   U (as in rune)
Movement   blue
Feeling   yellow
Character   lilac

6   B
Movement   yellow
Feeling   blue
Character   red

7 Ch
Movement   orange
Feeling   green-blue
Character   dark violet

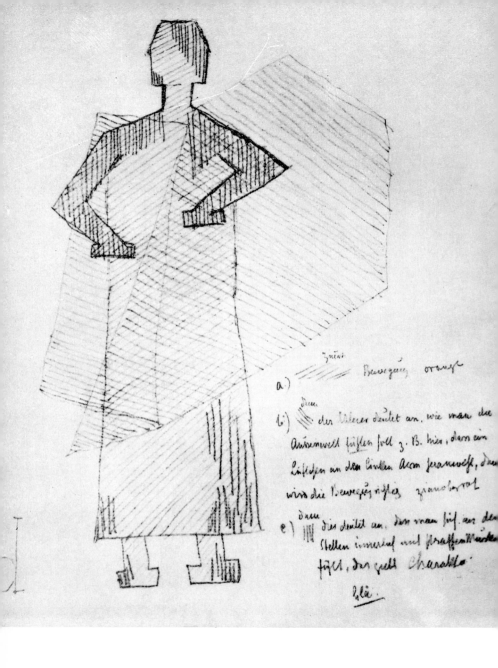

8   D
Movement   orange
Feeling   vermilion
Character   lilac

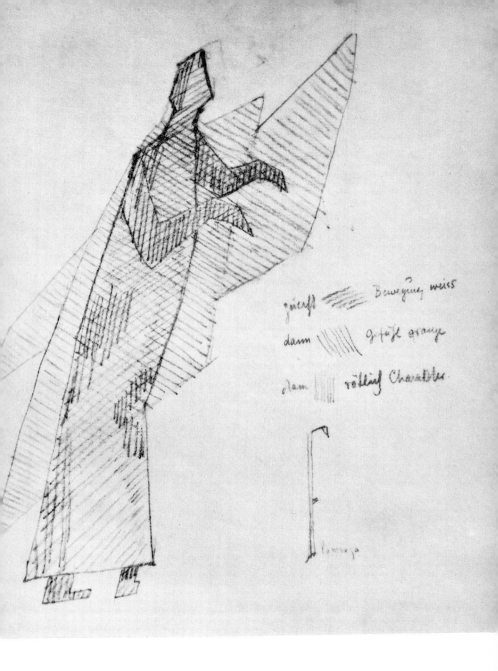

9   F
Movement   white
Feeling   orange
Character   reddish

10   G
Movement
Feeling
Character

yellow
silver-grey
blue

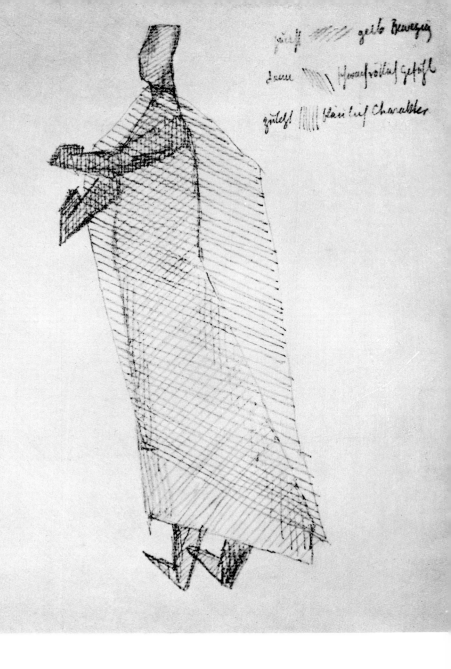

11   H
Movement   yellow
Feeling   pale-reddish
Character   blue-ish

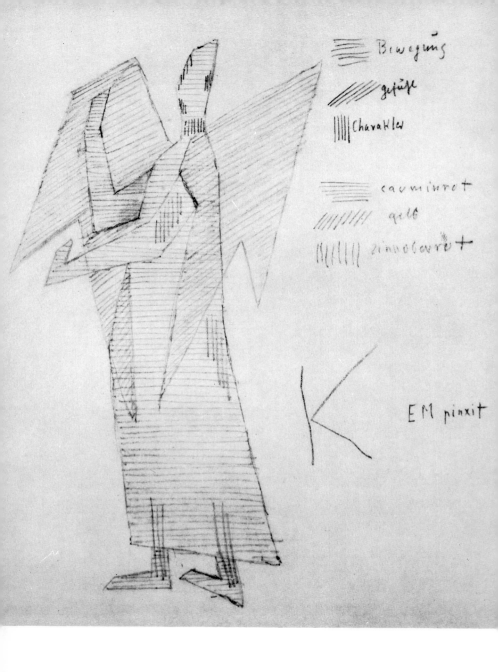

12   K
Movement   carmine red
Feeling   yellow
Character   vermilion

13   L
Movement   silver-grey
Feeling   lilac
Character   orange

14   M
Movement   green
Feeling   blue
Character   violet

15   N
Movement   yellow-green
Feeling   blue-violet
Character   lilac

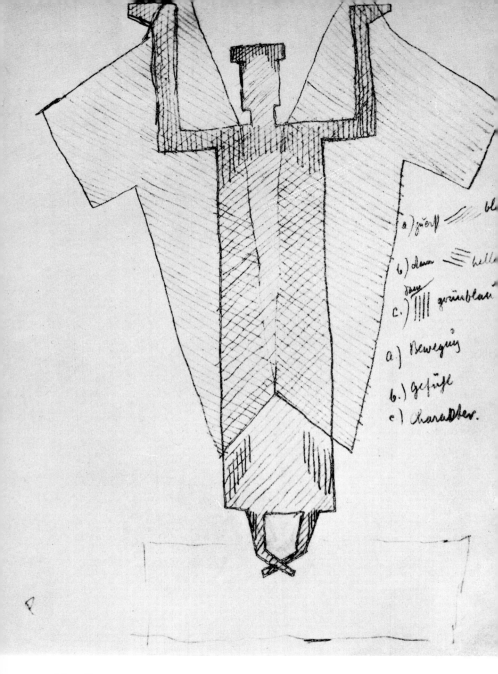

16   P
Movement   blue
Feeling   light lilac-red
Character   green-blue

17   R
Movement   red
Feeling   yellow
Character   green

18   S
Movement   grey
Feeling   brown
Character   black

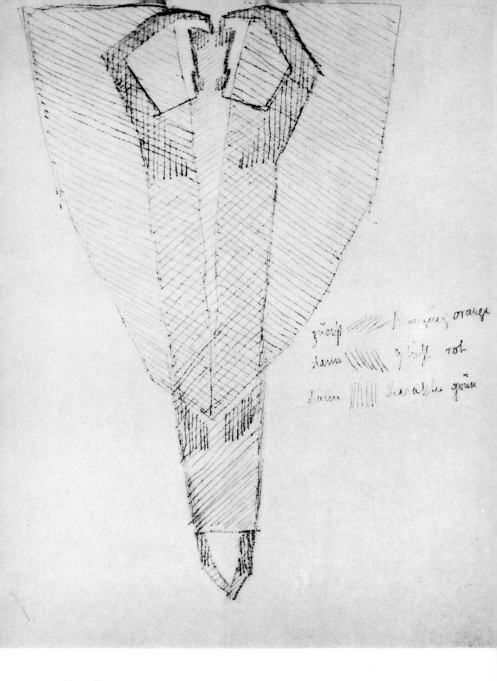

19   T
Movement   orange
Feeling   red
Character   green

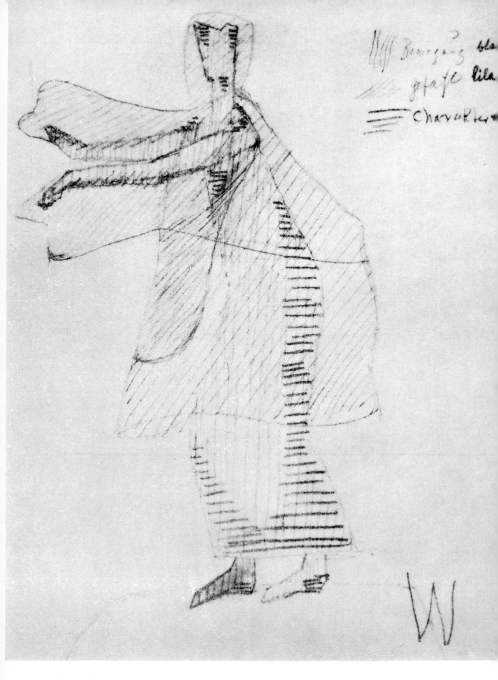

20   V
Movement   blue
Feeling   lilac
Character   red

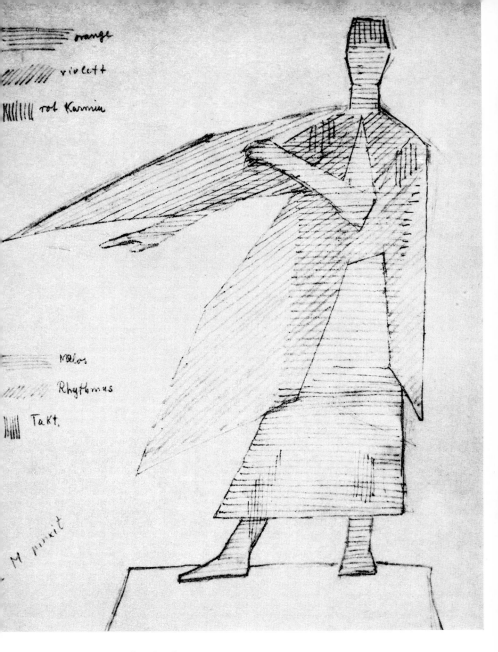

21   The major chord
Melody   orange
Rhythm   violet
Beat   carmine red

49

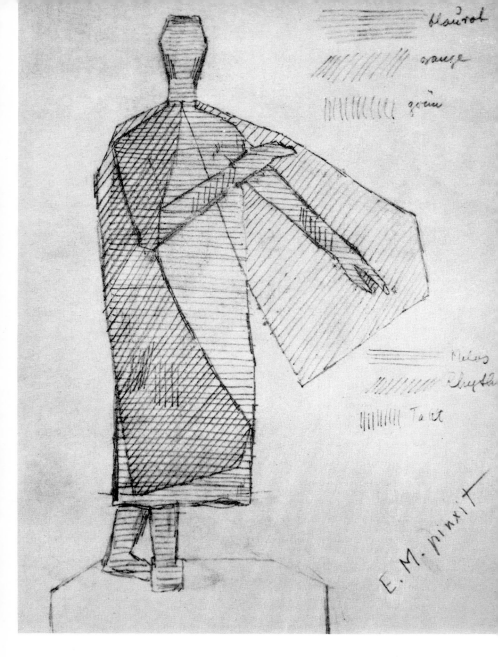

22 Minor chord
Melody   blue-red
Rhythm   orange
Beat   green

23   Self-assertion, almost megalomania
Movement   green
Sense of vitality   red
Characteristic temperament   black

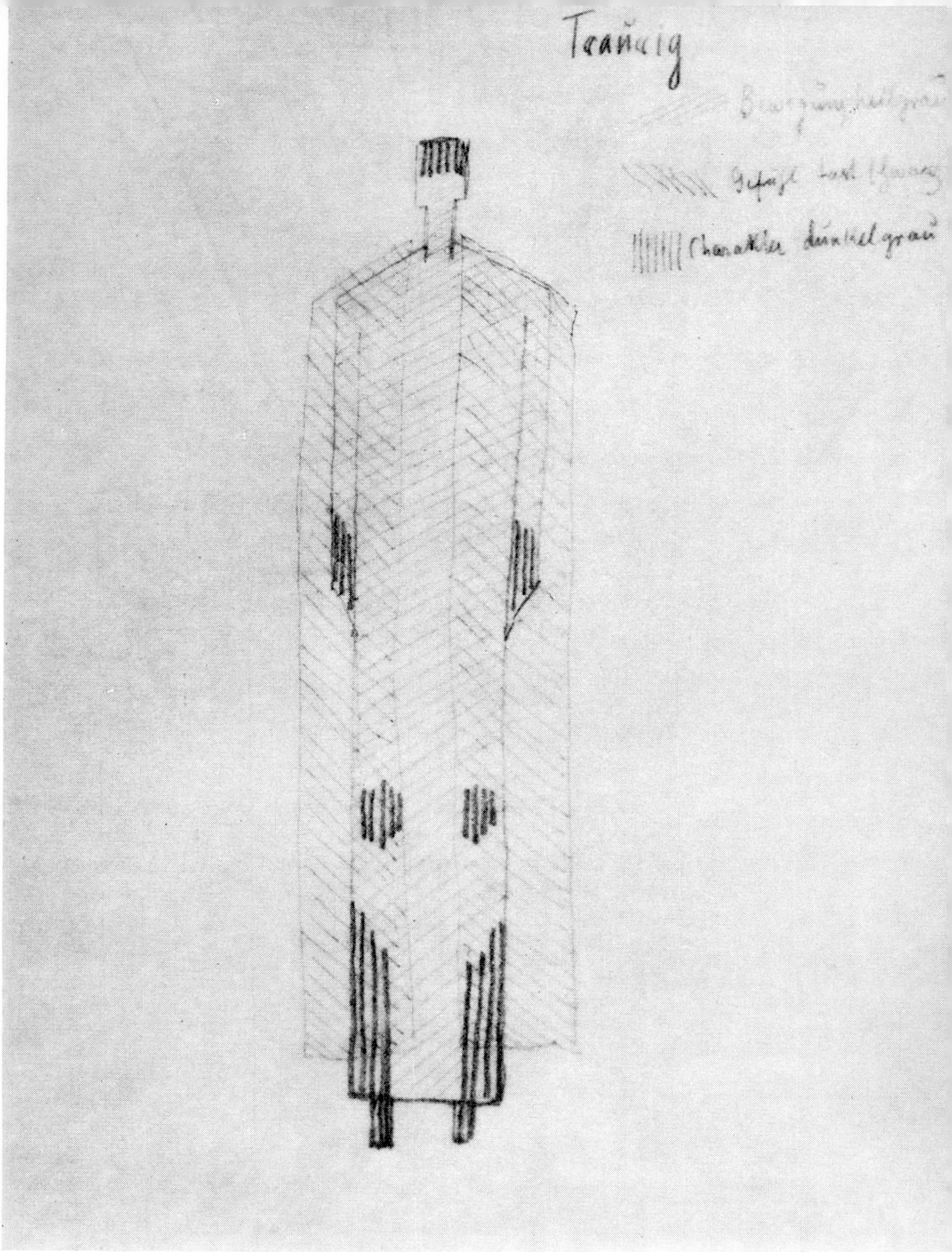

Trauaig

Bewegung hellgrau

Gefühl fast schwarz

Charakter dunkelgrau

24   Grief
Movement   light grey
Feeling   nearly black
Character   dark grey

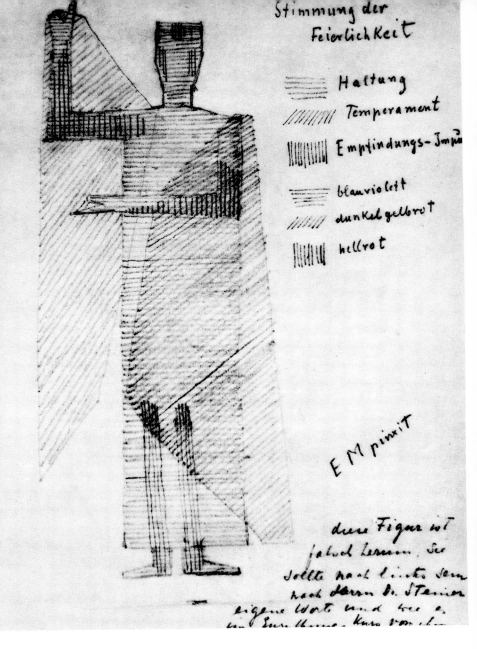

25 Mood of high festival
          This figure should be reversed from left to right

Bearing   blue-violet
Temperament   dark yellow-red
Impulse of feeling   light red

53

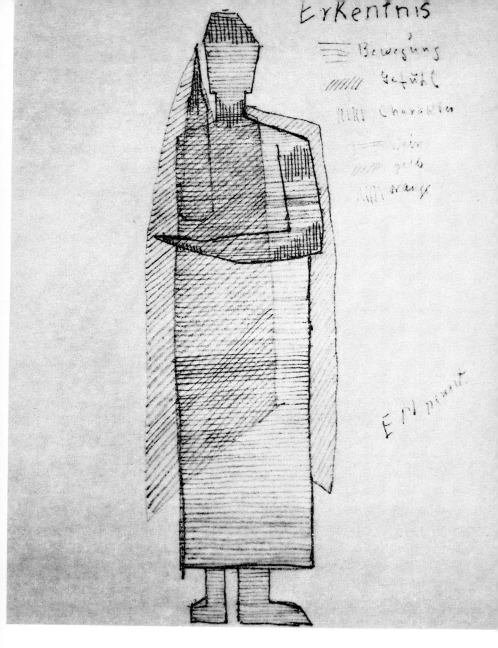

26   Knowledge
Movement   white
Feeling   yellow
Character   orange

54

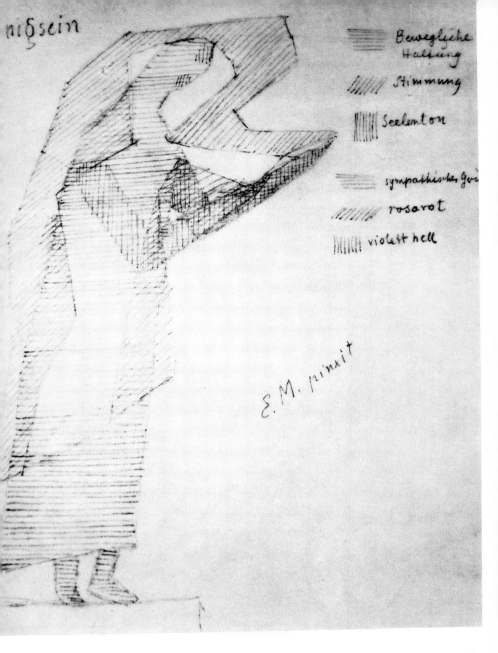

27   Inwardness
Mobility of bearing   gentle green
Mood   rose red
Quality of soul   light violet

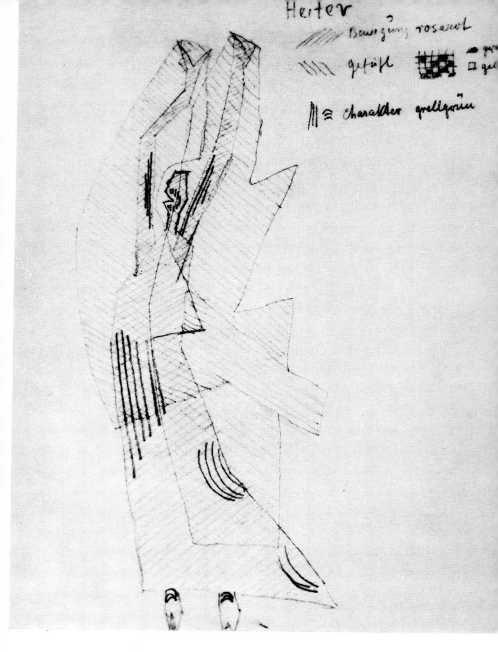

28   Merriment
Movement
Feeling
Character

rose red
■ green □ yellow mottled.
harsh green

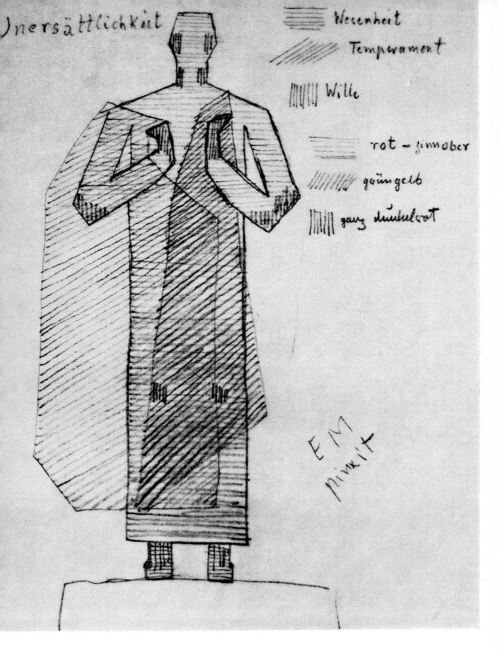

Jnersättlichkeit

Wesenheit
Temperament
Wille

rot – zinnober
grüngelb
ganz dunkelrot

EM
pinxit

29   Greed
Being   vermilion red
Temperament   green yellow
Will   really dark red

30   Despair
Movement   grey-blue
Gesture   blue
Perplexity   white-yellow

31   Loveableness
Movement and mobility   light rose-red
Mood   yellow
Freshness of soul   Somewhat darker rose-red

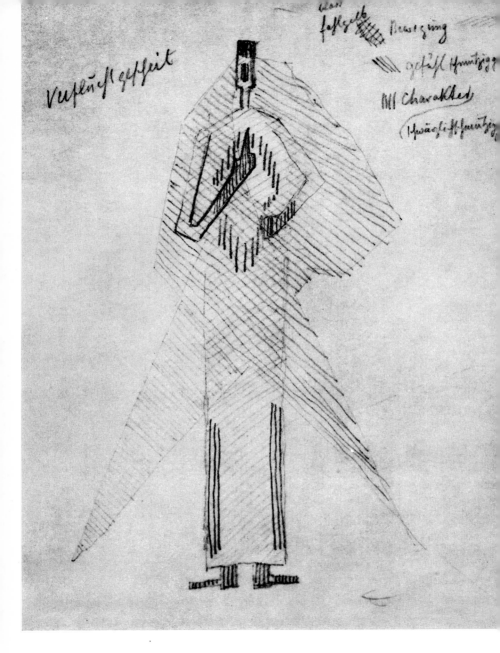

32   Damn clever
Movement   pale yellow
Feeling   dirty green
Character   blackish dirty grey

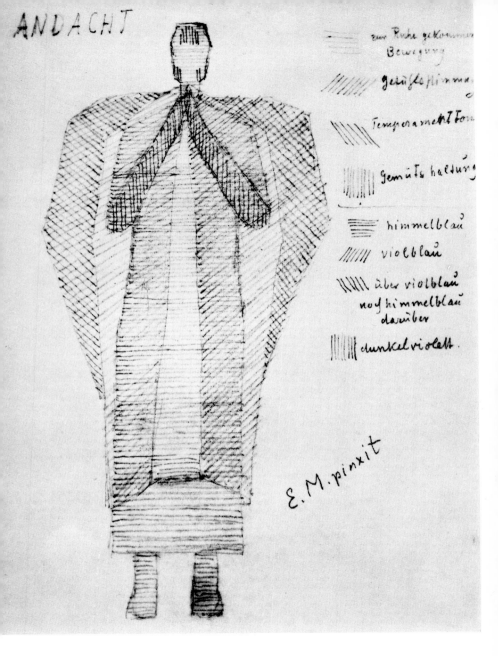

ANDACHT

zur Ruhe gekommen
Bewegung

gefühlsstimmung

Temperament Form

Gemüts haltung

himmelblau

violblau

über violblau
noch himmelblau
darüber

dunkel violett.

E. M. pinxit

33   Devotion
Movement come to rest   sky blue
Mood of feeling   violet blue
Nuance of temperament   sky blue over violet blue
Inner bearing   dark violet

34   Communication

Bearing   yellow
Will withheld   violet
Eagerness   red

35   Question—to be used wherever question or doubt arises
Gesture   light yellow
Feeling   greenish
Character   grey violet